An Eye
for Color

An Eye for Color

The Story of Josef Albers

Natasha Wing
Art by Julia Breckenreid

Henry Holt and Company ▪ New York

Henry Holt and Company, LLC
Publishers since 1866
175 Fifth Avenue
New York, New York 10010
www.HenryHoltKids.com

This book is the independent work written and illustrated by Natasha Wing and Julia Breckenreid
and is not endorsed or sponsored by the Josef and Anni Albers Foundation.

Library of Congress Cataloging-in-Publication Data
Wing, Natasha.
An eye for color : the story of Josef Albers / Natasha Wing ; illustrated by Julia Breckenreid.—1st ed.
p.   cm.
Includes bibliographical references.
ISBN: 978-0-8050-8072-8
1. Albers, Josef—Juvenile literature. 2. Artists—Germany—Biography—Juvenile literature.
3. Color in art—Juvenile literature. 4. Picture books for children. I. Breckenreid, Julia. II. Title.
N6888.A5W45 2009   709.2—dc22   2008038214

First Edition—2009 / Designed by Véronique Lefèvre Sweet
The artist used gouache on Arches Cover to create the illustrations for this book.
Printed in April 2010 in China by South China Printing Company Ltd.,
Dongguan City, Guangdong Province, on acid-free paper. ∞

3 5 7 9 10 8 6 4 2

Josef Albers saw art in the simplest things.

Growing up in a coal-mining city in Germany, he watched
his father paint doors as if they were artists' canvases.

As a poor student, he mined scraps from the dump and turned them into collages that shined like jewels.

When he became an art teacher, he experimented with glass and optical illusions.

In 1933, Josef was invited to teach in America. His goal was "to open eyes." "Watch what's going on," he told his students, "and capture the accident."

Although he found simple beauty in America, it was Mexico that captured his eye. The buildings! The pottery! The way colors looked different under the Mexican sun fascinated him. He wrote to a fellow artist, "Mexico is truly the promised land of abstract art."

During one visit, he made a series of abstract paintings inspired by adobe buildings. Their flat roofs and smooth, sun-dried mud surfaces were both simple and bold. Over and over again, Josef painted nothing but rectangles. Long rectangles. Tall rectangles. Rectangles within rectangles—all in different combinations of colors.

Interesting effects emerged!
When he changed the colors of the rectangles, the mood
of the painting changed.

Some paintings felt happy.

Others quiet.

Colors themselves changed. Blue looked different
next to orange . . .

. . . than it did next to beige.

Color was not what it first appeared to be. *But why? What else could it do?*

Determined to learn more, he set out to study color as carefully as a scientist. He started in the simplest way possible.

In 1949, at the age of sixty-one, Josef began his exploration.

First, he chose one shape, the most geometrically perfect shape: the square. Next, he picked the purest form of color: paint straight from the tube, no mixing.

Last, there would be no overlapping of colors, just colors side by side.

He painted squares within squares of different sizes and colors.

Colors came to life like actors on a stage!
One color stepped away.

Another popped forward.

Colors became

softer and **LOUDER.**

The yellow is the same in both squares,
only the background has changed.

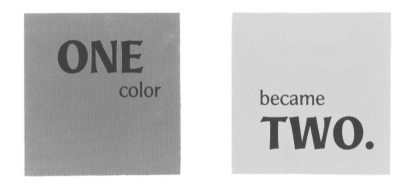

ONE color became **TWO.**

The green is the same in both squares,
only the background has changed.

Or changed into its opposite.

Stare at this square   Now look here!
for 30 seconds.

Colors even

DISAPPEARED!

Josef kept making painting after painting of squares. With each painting he proved that colors don't stand alone—they interact!

"I can kill the most brilliant red by putting it with violet," he said.

"I can make the dullest gray in the world dance by setting it against black."

Josef put his findings into a book, *Interaction of Color*. It changed the way the art world looked at color and the way teachers taught art.

The Metropolitan Museum of Art in New York recognized the importance of Josef's study. It was the first time the museum ever gave a living artist a one-man show of his life's work.

For twenty-seven years, Josef created images of squares—more than a thousand of them! For him, there was no end to what he could learn about color.

"I'm not paying 'homage to a square,' " said Josef. "It's only
the dish I serve my craziness about color in."

Today, his squares hang in art galleries around the world,
showing that color alone—as simple as it is—can be an exciting
form of art.

■ Author's Note ■

When I was a young girl living in Orange, Connecticut, Josef Albers was my neighbor.

As a child, I didn't know how important he was. All I knew was that he was a kind, old man who walked in my neighborhood, wearing a long overcoat and a beret. He always stopped to talk to the kids. And he loved my German shepherd, Nicky.

My mom told me he was an artist. So to show off our own artistic talents, my sister and I made a gift for him—a giant HI made of small pinecones glued to a wood board. We presented it to him with great pride. He accepted it with a shy smile. We felt so special!

I started taking art classes at school. One day I met him on one of his walks. I was heading home, carrying a canvas in my hand. It was a painting I was working on of a deer lying in a clearing by the woods. Mr. Albers asked to see it. While he inspected it, I held my breath, hoping for his approval.

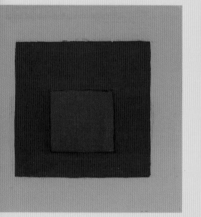   

"Very good," he said with his German accent. "Very good, Natasha."

That day I must have skipped home believing that I, too, could be an artist.

One year he sent my family a Christmas card. It had red squares. I thought, *What's the big deal about red squares? That's easy to paint.* My mother framed his card, so I knew that he had to be famous. She never framed anyone else's cards.

After I had grown up and moved away, I saw paintings in galleries that looked like our Christmas card. I read the name by the painting. Josef Albers. My old neighbor!

It was a number of years later that I began to wonder again, *Why are these squares important?*

So I read books and went online and learned about Josef Albers. I even visited the Josef and Anni Albers Foundation in Connecticut to study his paintings. I discovered his squares were part of a series of paintings he called Homage to the Square. He was so fascinated with color that he devoted twenty-seven years of his life to painting squares just to learn more about color.

Now when I see his colored squares in art galleries, I think about how lucky I was to have had such a talented and influential neighbor.

Josef Albers at his house in Orange, Connecticut, in 1971.

Jon Naar

■ More About Josef Albers ■

"In order to use color effectively it is necessary to recognize that color deceives continually." —Josef Albers

Josef Albers was born in Bottrop, Germany, on March 19, 1888. His father was a handyman. Young Josef enjoyed watching his father work and learned from him, as he said, by "stealing with the eyes."

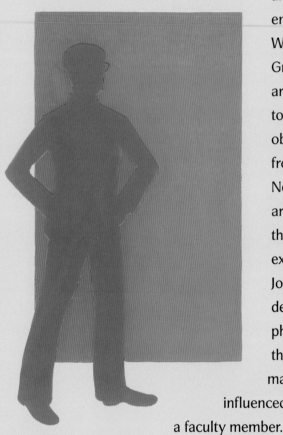

In his early twenties, Josef became a primary school teacher. Later he was certified as an art teacher. In 1920, at the age of thirty-two, he entered the Bauhaus, a school of design in Weimar, Germany, that was founded by Walter Gropius in 1919. The Bauhaus philosophy was that art, technology, and business should be brought together to apply good design to industrial objects, such as buildings and furniture. Artists from Germany, Russia, Switzerland, and the Netherlands developed an International Style of architecture and design. The school encouraged the use of modern technology and materials, as it explored new ways to make art and architecture. Josef did glass painting, metalwork, furniture design, and typography. He also was a photographer. Walter Gropius believed that nothing more than a balance of solids and space was needed to make something beautiful. This belief obviously influenced Josef who was first a student of Bauhaus, then a faculty member.

Josef was an unusual teacher. He didn't use books. Instead, he encouraged his students to use their eyes and hands. With cardboard, wire mesh, ribbons, newspapers, and stones, his students learned to see the beauty of everyday things.

When the Bauhaus was closed by the Nazis in 1933, Josef came to America to head the art department at the experimental Black Mountain College near Asheville, North Carolina. He taught there until 1949. He and his wife, Anni, took many trips to Mexico during this time. It was in Mexico that Josef did a series of repetitive paintings called *Adobe* or *Variant*, based on the adobe buildings he saw.

From 1950 to 1958, he was the head of the design department at Yale University in New Haven, Connecticut. About 1949, when Josef was sixty-one years old, he started his study of color, which he called Homage to the Square. The artist's approach to painting was very methodical, doing practice painting after practice painting of squares in various sizes and colors until he narrowed down the colors he wanted to paint. Wearing clean beige pants and a white shirt, Josef would slowly spread the paint with a palette knife onto Masonite. Remembering something his father told him as a child, he started with the center square and worked his way out, careful not to get his cuffs dirty. He used warm and cool colors, muted and intense colors to see what optical effects, or tricks to the eye, they would have on the viewer. Josef's Homage to the Square study continued for twenty-seven years.

Josef's paintings also used the effect of afterimages. When a viewer looked away from a painting, he would still see an illusion of the image.

On the back of every painting, Josef listed the colors he used.

Although his method seemed more scientific than artistic, he said, "Science aims at solving the problems of life, whereas art depends on unsolved problems." He considered each finished painting a variant rather than a final solution, leaving room for endless experimentation.

Not only was Josef a painter but he was also interested in printmaking, murals, photography, glass fusing and etching, and architecture. He published articles, poetry, and books on art. In 1963, after he retired from Yale University, he published a book, *Interaction of Color*, about his findings on color and the experiments he and his students did in the classroom. This book made him famous as a teacher and changed the way other teachers taught art and how students learned about color.

As a writer and a teacher, Josef influenced young artists, including Robert Rauschenberg and Neil Welliver. He was an original member of the American Abstract Artists. In 1971, he was the first living artist ever to be the subject of a solo exhibition at the Metropolitan Museum of Art.

Josef lived in Orange, Connecticut, until his death on March 25, 1976, at the age of eighty-eight, at which time he was still painting squares. In 1980, a postage stamp with one of his red paintings from Homage to the Square was issued with the words LEARNING NEVER ENDS.

■ Glossary ■

AFTERIMAGE The ghost image of the object a person stares at. The afterimage takes on the complementary color of the real object.

ANALOGOUS COLORS Colors next to each other on the color wheel, such as red and orange. Also known as adjacent colors.

COLOR What eyes see when light bounces off an object. Color is made up of hue, value, and intensity.

COLOR WHEEL A circular map of the colors. It shows the relationship between colors.

COMPLEMENTARY COLORS Colors opposite each other on the color wheel, such as blue and orange.

COOL COLORS Blue, green, and violet.

HUE The name for the light waves we see: red, orange, yellow, green, blue, and violet, which make up the spectrum.

INTENSE COLORS Strong colors that are pure and tend to cause emotional feelings; for example, yellow creates feelings of joy and happiness.

INTENSITY Brightness or dullness of a color.

MUTED COLORS Bright colors that have been dulled, usually with their complementary color.

NEUTRAL COLORS Black, white, and gray. To darken a color to make a shade, add black; for example, burgundy is a shade of red. To lighten a color to make a tint, use white; pink is a tint of red.

PIGMENT Dry, crushed substance, which when added to a liquid makes colored paint.

PRIMARY COLORS Red, yellow, and blue. These are the only colors you can't make by mixing colors. Instead, they are used to make other colors.

SECONDARY COLORS Orange, green, and violet. Each is a mixture of two primary colors. Their hue is halfway between the two primary colors that were used to mix them.

SPECTRUM The band of colors produced when sunlight is passed through a prism.

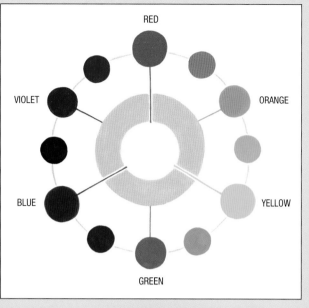

Color wheel

TERTIARY COLORS	Red-orange, red-violet, yellow-orange, yellow-green, blue-green, and blue-violet. These hues are made by mixing a primary color with a secondary color next to it on the color wheel. The tertiary colors are located between the primary and secondary colors they are made from.
VALUE	Lightness or darkness of a color.
WARM COLORS	Red, orange, and yellow.

■ Selected Bibliography ■

Albers, Josef. *Interaction of Color.* New Haven: Yale University Press, 1963.

———. *Search Versus Re-Search: Three Lectures by Joseph Albers at Trinity College, April 1965.* Hartford, Conn.: Trinity College Press, 1969.

Danilowitz, Brenda. *The Prints of Joseph Albers: A Catalogue Raisonné, 1915–1976.* New York: Hudson Hills Press, 2001.

Solomon R. Guggenheim Museum (New York). *Josef Albers: A Retrospective.* New York: Harry N. Abrams, 1988.

See-for-Yourself Activities

Material needed for the following activities:

- Construction paper in different colors, including red, yellow, black, white, violet, gray
- Scissors
- Ruler
- Black marker
- White background, such as a wall, large poster board, large painter's canvas, or white board (chalkboard)

RED SQUARES

Cut two small squares out of the same piece of red paper. Make sure they are the same size. Then cut out a big yellow square and a big black square, both the same size. Put a small red square in the center of the yellow square, and a small red square in the center of the black square. Does the red still look like the same color? Or does one now look more orange?

DULL AND DANCING

Put a small red square on a larger piece of white paper. Notice how brilliant it is. Now put it on a piece of violet paper. Does it change? Put a gray square on a piece of white paper. Now put it on a piece of black paper. Does it seem to jump out now?

PRESTO CHANGO!

Cut out a red circle, about 3 inches across. Put a tiny black dot in the middle. Put the red circle in the middle of a big piece of black paper. Stare at the black dot in the center of the small red circle. Slowly count to 30. Quickly look at a white background, such as a wall or a blank piece of white paper. What color do you see now?

SUBTRACTING COLOR

Put three different color squares on a white background. How many colors do you see, not including the background? Three! Now put the three squares on a background that's the same color as one of the colors. Now how many colors do you see, not including the background? What happened to the third color?

OPEN YOUR EYES

Cut out different geometric shapes from colored paper. Think of what you learned about color, and create your own art!